# STICKER STORIES
# FAIRY TALE
*Adventures*

Walter Foster
Jr.

*Illustrated by Nila Aye*
*Written by Samantha Chagollan*

# How to Use This Book

It's easy to create your own stories
with stickers and drawings of your
fairy tale friends!

Here's what
you need:

- This book
- Blank drawing paper
- Pencils, an eraser,
  and crayons
- Your imagination!

Eraser

# Here's what you do:

**1** *Make a Scene*
Fill up the story pages with stickers to complete the scenes.

**2** *Draw It Out*
Follow the simple steps to draw your own characters.

**3** *Tell a Story*
Combine stickers and drawings to make your own adventures, starting with the scene on page 24!

Princess Penelope is puckering
up to kiss this frog. Will he turn into
a prince or something else?

Add some stickers to show
what happens next!

# frog

Start with two half ovals that look like the letter "M." Add two circles for eyes and a big circle for the body.

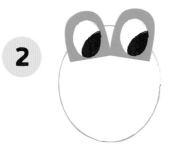

Now draw the front and back legs, and give him a big, fly-catching grin!

# prince

Draw an oval for his face, and add his crown with three yellow triangles.

Draw his body and legs with rectangles, and give him a fancy suit and boots!

# Captain Salty has dropped anchor for a beach party. Can you help him celebrate?

Ahoy, matey! Add stickers to
help him play in the sand.

# treasure chest

Draw a rectangle first, and then add a smaller rectangle inside and a square for the lock.

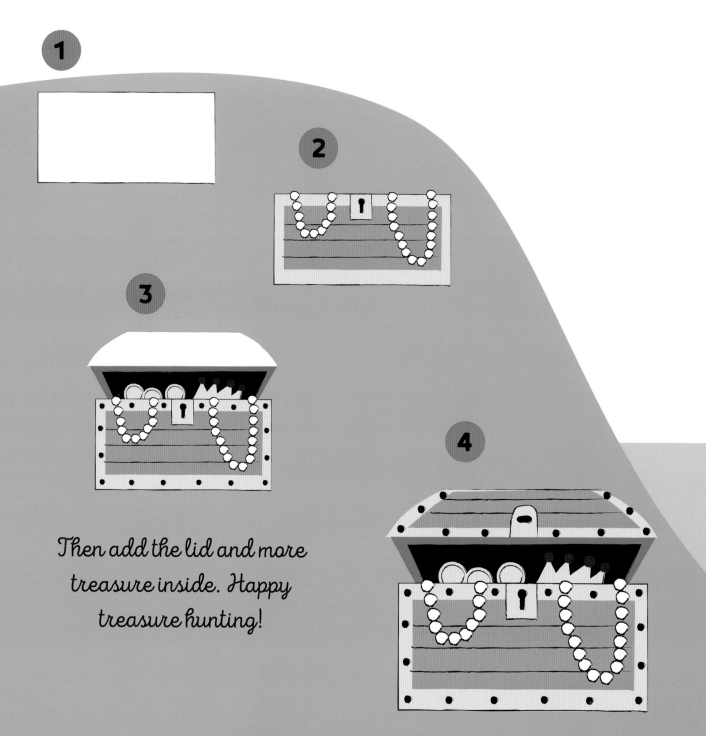

Then add the lid and more treasure inside. Happy treasure hunting!

# pirate ship

Begin with the outline of the ship
and the circle windows.

Draw curved rectangles
for the sails, and fly
a fierce flag.

It's a beautiful day under the rainbow!
Dazzle the unicorn is excited to
play with her best friends.

Add some friends for
Dazzle to play with!

# unicorn

Draw the outline of the unicorn's head
and body, then add the legs, mane,
and tail.

Add the other two legs, and then add the hooves and majestic horn!

**5**

**6**

**7**

# fairy

Draw the fairy's face first,
then add her pink dress and legs.

**6**

Now draw her wings and arms and a wand for granting wishes!

**7**

The king and queen
are visiting from another
kingdom. Who has come
to welcome them?

Add stickers to show who wants to
meet the king and queen!

On his quest, Brave Sir Rupert
meets a fire-breathing dragon.
Will he save the princess?

Who will help him in his quest?
Make a scene with some stickers!

# castle

Start with a square, and then add rectangles, triangles, and more squares.

1

2

3

4

*Include lots of details, like windows, flags, and stones, to make it look like the real thing!*

# princess

Give this lovely princess a beautiful gown
to wear using curved lines.

*Draw long, wavy lines for her
hair. Add a crown too!*

Sticker and draw your own fairy tale adventure!